Animal Peculiarity

By T.P Just

~~~

Get All The Books In The Series:

Table of Contents

1 Introduction

The unique characteristics of animals is a miscellany of facts, genuine or supposed, gleamed from earlier and contemporary Greek writers (No Latin writer is once named) and to a limited extent from his own observation to illustrate the habits of the animal world.

We are of course prepared to encounter much that modern science rejects, but the general tone with its search after the picturesque, the startling, even the miraculous, would justify us in ranking Aelian with the paradoxical, rather than with the sober exponents of natural history.

Mythology, mariners' yarns, vulgar superstitions, the ascertained facts of nature—all serve to adorn a tale and, on occasion, to point a moral. His religion is the popular stoicism of the age. Aleian repeatedly affirms his belief in the gods and in divine providence; the wisdom and beneficence of Nature are held up to veneration; the folly and selfishness of man are contrasted with the untaught virtues of the animal world.

Some animals, to be sure, have their failings, but he chooses rather to dwell upon their good qualities, devotion, courage, self-sacrifice, gratitude. Again, animals are guided by reason, and from them we may learn contentment, control of the passions, and calm in the face of death.

His primary object is to entertain and while so doing to convey instruction in the most agreeable form. Some might find fault with his random and piece-meal handling of his theme-of which he is well aware, and he defends himself with the plea that a frequent change of topic helps to maintain the reader's interest and saves him from boredom.

As to the permanent value of his work he has no misgivings and since we have been informed that his writings were much admired, we may assume that they appealed to cultivated circles in a way that the voluminous and possibly arid compilations of grammarians did not.

2.Animal Courage

Men have need of the spoken word to stimulate and persuade them to be good, to banish cowardice, to gather courage : athletes, with a view to running; soldiers, with a view to fighting. Animals however need no extraneous encouragement but stimulate their prowess for themselves and rouse and incite themselves.

For instance, the Boar when intending to do battle whets his tusks on smooth rocks. Homer, you know, gives clear evidence touching the animal. Further, the Lion rouses himself by lashing himself with his tail and allows no idling and no repose.

And this poet knew when he spoke of the Lion. And Elephants inflame themselves for the fight, whenever the occasion arises, by beating themselves with their trunk: they need no one to sing to them and say 'This is no time for sitting still or for delaying, still less do they wait for the poems of Tyrtaeus.

3 The Bull in Defeat

And when a Bull that is the leader of a herd is defeated by another leader, he departs to some other place and becomes his own trainer and practices every method of fighting, scattering the dust over himself and rubbing his horns against tree-trunks and fitting himself in other ways to display his Strength, and particularly abstaining from sexual acts and living continently like Iccus of Tarentum, whom Plato the son of Ariston celebrates as refraining from all sexual commerce during the entire period of the Games.

Now to Iccus, who was a man and who loved the Olympic and Pythian games and who understood what glory was and who longed for fame, it was no great matter to restrain himself and to spend the nights continently. For to him the prizes meant glory-the wild olive of, Olympia, the Isthmian pine, and the Pythian laurel, admiration in his lifetime, and after death an honored name.

Again, the harper Amoebeus, I am told, married a woman of surpassing beauty but had no intercourse with her when he was going to the theatre in order to compete there. And Diogenes the actor in tragedies eschewed absolutely all licentious unions. And Clitomachus the pancratiast, if ever he saw dogs coupling, would turn away; and if at a Wine party he heard some licentious and bawdy story, would get up and leave.

There is nothing surprising that being men they should behave so, either in order to make money or to achieve renown and fame. But, Q son of Ariston, when a bull overcomes his adversary, what proclamation announces his victory, and what prizes do men award him?

4 A Tame Leopard

Brute beasts are in the habit of not molesting their companions and of frequently sparing them,

For instance, I have heard the following story. A hunter had a Leopard which he had tamed from its earliest days and which he loved and tended assiduously as though it were his friend or darling.

Now he brought a kid and gave it to the Leopard alive, thinking to provide it at once with food and with the pleasure of tearing the kid to pieces, and supposing that it would refuse to eat dead meat. In fact when the kid was brought the Leopard controlled itself: being full-fed it needed to abstain from food.

And it did the same on the second day, for it still needed the medicine of starvation. But when the third day came it began to grow hungry and, as usual, showed that it was by the sound of its voice; for all that, it still would not touch the kid which had been its friend for two days, but left it alone, though it accepted another one. Men however have betrayed even their brothers and their parents and old friends; there have been many and frequent cases.

5 The Bear

I have described in some earlier passage "how the Bear produces some shapeless flesh and then licks it into shape and, so to say, moulds it. But what I have not already mentioned I will mention now, and this is a suitable occasion.

It gives birth in the winter time, and having done so, hibernates; and as it dreads the frosts it awaits the coming of spring, and would never bring its cubs out until three full months have passed. But when it perceives that it is pregnant it dreads this as though it were some sickness, and seeks for a lair.

(Hence the Bear's hibernation is called its 'lair period.') Then it enters, not on its feet but lying down, thus effacing its tracks for those who hunt it, for it drags itself along on its back. And having entered, it rests, and in some way reduces its figure; and this it does for forty days. Aristotle however says that the Bear remains motionless and does not stir for fourteen days, and for the remainder she just turns.

So she passes the entire forty days without food or nourishment: it is enough for her to lick her right paw. And owing to excessive colliquescence her intestines become wrinkled up and compressed. Knowing this, as soon as she emerges she eats some of the plant called ' wild arum and as this induces flatulence, it opens up her gut, widens it, and renders it capable of admitting food.

And when she has filled herself out once more, she eats some ants and obtains an easy evacuation I have now sufficiently described how Bears empty and fill their bodies by natural means without any need, my fellow men, of doctors or of concoctions.

6 The Snake, its diet of poison

When Snakes intend to eat fruit they swallow the juice of the herb called picris. It helps to prevent them from being filled with Wind. And when they intend to lie in Wait for a human being or an animal, they eat poisonous roots and herbs too of the same description.

So it seems that Homer too was aware of what they ate. For instance, he tells how a Snake waits for a man, lying coiled up near its lurking—place, after it has taken its fill of much poisonous, deadly provender.

7 The Stag and its antlers

When Deer have cast their antlers they go and hide in coverts and so protect themselves against attackers; and rightly so, for as they are without means of self-defence they are convinced that they have for the time being lost their strength.

It is said also that, while the stumps are still fresh and before they have hardened and the young horns, called chondroi, have begun to form, they take care that the sun's rays shall not fall upon them and cause the flesh to putrefy.

8 The Horse in Battle

When Horses march to battle they become suspicious at having to Jump trenches, at having to leap over pits and to pass through stakes and palisades and the like. And one finds Homer saying about such matters

Thus Hector passing through the throng implored his comrades, urging them to cross the trench. But even his swift horses dared not, but neighed loudly as they stood upon the sheer brink, for the yawning trench dismayed them, not easy to leap from close up, nor to cross.

9 The Crow Of King Mares

In Egypt near the lake Moeris as it is called, where Crocodilopolis is, the tomb of a Crow is pointed out. The Egyptians give the following reason. The King of Egypt (Mares was his name) possessed a remarkable Crow which was quite tame.

Any dispatches that he wished to have delivered any where this Crow would speedily carry; and it was the swiftest of messengers: having heard its destination, it knew where it must direct its flight to, which spot it must pass, and where it must pause on arrival. In reward for these services Mares honoured it when dead with a monument and a tomb.

10 The Bear and Its Cubs

Every animal has a special word to denote the care spent on its upbringing. For example, one might speak of the ' breaking in of horses, the 'rearing' of hounds, the ' grooming ' of elephants, the ' rearing ' of lions, the ' rearing ' of birds, and so forth.

Now here the Bear shows its clever tricks. If it is pursued together with its cubs it pushes them along in front as far as it is able. But when it realises that they are exhausted, it carries one on its back and another in its mouth, then laying hold of a tree, climbs up. And one cub clings to its back with its claws, while the other is carried in the teeth of the Bear as it mounts.

If when famished it comes across a bull, it does not engage in a straightforward battle of strength, but wrestles with it and seizing its neck brings it down and tightens its clench. And while the bull is being crushed it bellows, until at last, it gives up and lies dead; and the Bear takes its fill.

11 Docility of Certain Animals

Here is further evidence to show that animals are apt at learning. Egyptians taught baboons their letters, how to dance, how to play the flute and the harp. And a baboon would demand money for these accomplishments, and would put what was given him into a bag which he carried attached to his person, just like professional beggars.

It has long been noised abroad that the people of Sybaris have even taught horses how to dance, of the ease with which elephants can be induced to learn I have spoken above. Now dogs are capable of managing household affairs for those who have trained them, and for a poor man it is enough to have a dog as slave.

There are after all people who are without slaves even of this kind, among the Arabs for instance the Troglodytes, among the Libyans the Nomads, and among the Ethiopians all the lake-dwellers, people who have never learned to eat anything other than fish.

12 Memory in Animals

Animals retain the memory of their experiences and have no need of those mnemonic systems Devised by any other of those who have been extolled for their profession and their skill in this matter.

For instance, a cow goes to the spot where her calf was taken from her and mourns for it, lowing as is her wont. Some oxen too when about to be yoked express their pleasure, others draw back. And a horse on hearing the clash of curb-chain and the clang of bit, and seeing chest-plates and frontlets, begins" to snort and makes his hoofs ring as he prances, and is in an ecstasy. And the shouting of the stablemen stimulates him and he pricks up his ears and dilates his nostrils as he remembers his galloping and yearns irresistibly for his wonted exercise.

13 The Deer and Its Young

The Deer produces its young by the roadside and appears to do so from a wise precaution, because it dreads wild beasts and their designs, but has no fear of human beings: it knows full well that it is weaker than the former, but has no doubt that it can escape from the latter. But when it has grown fat it would no longer give birth by the roadside, for it knows that it is too sluggish to run, and so it brings forth its young in glens, in thickets, and in ravines.

The Deer its Frugality

The Deer (so I am told) is content with what is before it and has no further wants, but is more frugal than man in its appetite. For instance, in the neighborhood of the Hellespont there is a hill pastured by Deer, which have one of their ears cleft, and they do not stray beyond this hill, do not want strange food, desire no other meadows from any need of a larger amount of grass; so what is at hand is enough for them the whole year round.

14 The Hyena, its Narcotic Powers

The Hyena, has in its Left paw the power of sending to sleep and can with a mere touch induce torpor. For instance, it often visits stables, and when it finds any creature asleep it creeps softly up and puts what you might call its sleep-inducing paw upon the creature's nose, and it is suffocated and overpowered.

Meantime the Hyena scoops out the earth beneath the head to such a depth as makes the head bend back into the hole, leaving the throat uppermost and exposed. There upon it fastens on to the animal, throttles it, and carries it oft to its lair.

And it attacks dogs in the following manner. When the moon's disc is full, the Hyena gets the rays behind it and casts its own shadow upon the dogs and at once reduces them to silence, and having bewitched them, as sorceresses do, it then carries them off tongue—tied and thereafter puts them to such use as it pleases.

15 Dolphin and boy at Issus

The story of a Dolphin's love for a beautiful boy at Issus has long been celebrated, and I am determined not to leave it unrecorded; it shall accordingly be told.

The gymnasium at Issus is situated close to the sea, and after their running and their Wrestling the youths in accordance with an ancient custom go down there and wash themselves. Now while they were swimming about, a Dolphin fell passionately in love with a boy of remarkable beauty. At first when it approached, it frightened the boy and completely scared him; later on however, through constant meeting, it even led the boy to conceive a warm friendship and kindly feelings towards it.

For instance, they began to sport with one another; and sometimes they would compete, swimming side by side in rivalry, sometimes the boy would mount, like a rider on a horse, and be carried proudly along on the back of his lover. And to the people of Issus and to strangers the event seemed marvelous.

For the Dolphin would go a long way out to sea with its darling on its back and as far as it pleased its rider; than it would turn and bring, him close to the beach, and they would part company and return, the Dolphin to the open sea, the boy to his home. And the Dolphin used to appear at the hour when the gymnasium was dismissed, and the boy was delighted to find his friend expecting him and to play together. And besides his natural beauty, this too made him the admired of all, namely that not only men but even dumb animals thought him a boy of surpassing loveliness.

In a little while however even this mutual affection was destroyed by Envy. Thus, it happened that the boy exercised himself too vigorously, and in an exhausted state threw himself belly downwards on to his mount, and as the spike on the Dolphin's dorsal fin chanced to be erect it pierced the beautiful boy's navel. Whereupon certain veins were severed; there followed a gush of blood; and presently the boy died.

The Dolphin perceiving this from the weight for the boy lay heavier than usual, as he could not lighten himself by breathing—and seeing the surface of the Water crimson with blood, realized what had happened and could not bear to survive its darling.

And so with all the gathered force of a ship dashing through the waves it made its way to the beach and deliberately cast itself upon the shore, bringing the dead body with it. And there they both lay, the boy already dead, the Dolphin breathing its last.

16 Prophetic Powers Of Animals

Dogs, oxen, swine, goats, snakes, and other animals have a presentiment of an impending famine; they are the first to know when a pestilence or an earthquake is approaching. They can foretell fair weather and the fertility of the crops. Though devoid of reason, which can be a man's salvation or his destruction, they are not mistaken at any rate in the matters mentioned above.

The Snake, Its Veracity And Speed

Snakes, conscious that they have a narrow, elongated gullet, despite the fact that they are greedy and exceedingly voracious, rises upright and stands upon the tip of their tail, so that food slides down into them and passes into the bulk of their body. And having no feet they crawl at a great speed. Indeed one snake launches itself and flies with the speed of a javelin; and its name is derived from its action, for it is called Acontias (the Javelin-snake).

17 The Song Of Birds

Not one of the birds that sing and make melody has escaped observation, but we know that swallows, blackbirds, and the tribe of cicadas sing, that the jay is talkative, that the cricket buzzes, the locust makes a light strumming, the grasshopper is not silent, and moreover that halcyons and parrots are vocal, while among aquatic creatures the croak of the male frog is not silent.

And of these some utter a plaintive feminine note, others a note shrill and piercing; and some sing as they hurry from branch to branch, as though they were changing house, while others carol in the meadows as though they were holding festival, and while leading an existence that is, as it were, all flowers and delicacy.

Ability to Imitate Other Sounds

Now the jay can imitate all other sounds but especially the human voice. And the buff backed heron, as it is called, and the salpinx: (trumpet) and the Wryneck and the raven are peculiarly

fitted to imitate the following sounds. The buff-backed heron represents the neighing of a horse; the salpinx, the instrument whose name it bears; and the wryneck, the cross—flute; While the raven tries to imitate the sound of raindrops.

18 The Scorpion; Various Kind

The male Scorpion is exceedingly ferocious, but the female seems to be of a milder temper. And I have heard that there are eleven kinds: one is white, while another is red, another smoke-colour, there is also a black kind.

I have learned also that there is one kind that is green, another pot-bellied, and another that resembles a crab. But it is commonly said that the fiercest is the fiery colored one. I have also learned by report that there are Scorpions with wings and others with a double sting, and some-where one has been seen with seven vertebrae.

The Scorpion is not oviparous but viviparous. And it should be known that some say that the offspring of these creatures are not produced by mating but . . .heat causes Scorpions to be exceedingly prolific. And how they all inflict their sting, and the effect this produces, and how they kill, you will learn from another source.

19 Elephant and Python

In India, I am told, the Elephant and the Python are the bitterest enemies. Now Elephants draw down the branches of trees and feed upon them. And the Pythons, knowing this, crawl up the trees and envelop the lower half of their bodies in the foliage, but the upper portion extending to the head they allow to hang loose like a rope. And the Elephant approaches to pluck the twigs, where at the Python springs at its eyes and gouges them out.

Next the snake winds round, the Elephants neck, and [as it clings to the tree ?] with the lower part of its body, it tightens its hold with the upper part and strangles the Elephant with an unusual and singular noose.

Enmities and Fears Of Animals

To the lion, fire and a cock are utterly hateful; to the leopard a hyena, to the scorpion a gecko.

Thus, if the aforesaid creature is brought near to a scorpion, the latter is seized with numbness. And the elephant shrinks from the python; and every beast of burden dreads the shrew-mouse; the lobster, the octopus. Furthermore if you were to try to push dogs off the roof, you would not succeed in throwing them down: they are afraid of the great danger involved.

20 The Scorpion in Libya

What ingenuity, peculiar to their kind, Nature seems to have imparted to Scorpions! The people of Libya dreading their numbers and their machinations, devise endless schemes to counter them: they wear high boots; they sleep in beds raised high above the ground, setting their bed-cords away from the walls; they place the feet of their beds in vessels full of water, and imagine that they will thereafter sleep without fear and in peace.

But what tricks do the Scorpions devise! If a Scorpion can find some spot in the roof to which he can hang, he clings to it firmly with his claws and let's down his sting. Then a second descends from the roof, crawls down over the first, and with his claws holds fast to his sting and lets his own dangle in the air.

Then a third holds on to that, and a fourth on to the third, and a fifth in a line, while those that follow crawl down over the preceding ones. Then the last Scorpion strikes the sleeper; crawls up again over the one above; after him the next; then the third from the bottom; then the rest, until the entire lot is disconnected, just as if they had undone a chain.

21 The Fox and Hedge Hogs

The Fox is a crafty creature. For instance, it plots against Hedgehogs in the following way. It cannot overcome them by a direct attack, the reason being that their prickles prevent it; and so, gingerly and taking great care of its mouth, it turns them over and lays them on their back and after ripping them open, easily devours those whom till then it dreaded.

And Bustards

And this is the way that Foxes hunt Bustards in and Pontus. They reverse themselves and put their head down upon the ground and stick their tail up, like a bird's neck. And the bustards are taken in and approach, supposing it to be some bird of their own kind; then when they come close up, they are easily caught by the Fox, which turns upon them and attacks them violently.

And Small Fish

Their manner of catching very small fishes is extremely dexterous. They move along the bank of a stream and trail their tails in the water. And the fish swim up and are immersed and entangled in the thick hairs. When the Foxes notice this, they withdraw from the Water and go to dry ground where they shake their tails thoroughly: the little fishes tumble out, and the Foxes make a delicious meal.

Fox Tests Strength of Ice

The people of Thrace use this animal as an indicator of whether a frozen river is safe to cross. And if the Fox runs across without the ice bending or giving way beneath its tread, they make bold to follow. The Fox tests the safety of the transit in the following manner: it puts its ear down to the ice, and if it hears no sound of the flow beneath and no murmur in the depths, it has no fear, the ice being solid, and it races over without hesitation. Otherwise it would not set foot upon it.

22 The Monkey-Spider

The Monkey-spider has by some been called 'the mountain—ranger,' but by others (I am told) the wood-runner. It is born on trees and is hairy. It has also by some been called 'the flea.' Its belly has a slight incision, so that one might say it had been cut in two by a thread.

It inflicts the most dangerous bites, and they are attended by a trembling on the part of the victim; there ensues a sharp pain in the region of the heart; the urine is stopped; and the other passage also becomes blocked. It seems that the remedy for these afflictions is to eat a river-crab.

Get All The Books In The Series: